The New Novello Choral Edition
NOVELLO HANDEL EDITION

General Editor   Donald Burrows

LET GOD ARISE
CHAPEL ROYAL VERSION
(HWV 256b)

Anthem for Alto and Bass soloists, SATB chorus and orchestra

Edited by Donald Burrows

Vocal Score

NOVELLO PUBLISHING LIMITED
14 - 15 Berners Street, London, W1T 3LJ

It is requested that on all concert notices and programmes
acknowledgement is made to 'The Novello Handel Edition'.

*Es wird gebeten, auf sämtlichen Konzertankündigungen und
Programmen 'The Novello Handel Edition' als Quelle zu erwähnen.*

Il est exigé que toutes notices et programmes de concerts,
comportent des remerciements à 'The Novello Handel Edition'.

Permission to reproduce the Preface of this Edition must be obtained from the Publisher.

*Die Erlaubnis, das Vorwort dieser Ausgabe oder Teile desselben zu
reproduzieren, muß beim Verlag eingeholt werden.*

Le droit de reproduction de ce document à partir de la préface doit être obtenu de l'éditeur.

CONTENTS

Approximate duration
15 minutes

INSTRUMENTATION

Flute
Oboe
Bassoon
Strings
Continuo (Harpsichord or Organ)

The performing material for this edition
includes a fully-realised Continuo part.

PREFACE

On 25 February 1723 a warrant was issued from the Lord Chamberlain of the British court for the admission of Handel into the 'Place and Quality of Composer of Musick for his Majesty's Chappel Royal'. Although this was accompanied by a generous additional pension and carried a title comparable to a German *Kapellmeister*, the appointment was largely honorary and did not involve Handel in the daily routine of services. He did, however, have to fulfil one occasional duty by providing special music for the Sunday morning services in the Chapel Royal, St James's Palace, following King George I's return from visits to his Electorate in Hanover.[1] During the remainder of the King's reign there were just two such events, in January 1724 and January 1726, and the first of them was reported as follows in the London newspapers:

> Yesterday being the First Sunday after his Majesty's safe Arrival at St. James's, *Te Deum* and a fine New Anthem composed by the famous M. Handel, were performed both vocally and instrumentally at the Royal Chapel there by the greatest masters, before his Majesty and their Royal Highnesses.

The musical items were performed within the Anglican liturgy of Morning Prayer from the *Book of Common Prayer*, in which the Te Deum was one of the regular canticles and provision was made for the inclusion of an anthem.

Handel's anthems for the Chapel Royal services were recomposed from works that he had originally written for James Brydges's musicians at Cannons in 1717-18, the so-called 'Chandos Anthems'. The recomposition involved various elements, including adaptations to the vocal scoring: in that respect, the Chapel Royal choir was closer to modern choral practice than was Brydges's ensemble at Cannons. The circumstances of the Chapel Royal performances also influenced some features of the anthems: the King's private chapel was quite small, with opportunities for musical interplay between soloists, chorus and accompanying instruments, and the time-span was defined by the court timetable that required the Sunday morning service to be over in time for the King to dine 'in public'. Handel took a different path with each of the recompositions, mixing revisions of movements from previous works with new music. In the case of this anthem, the first and last movements were revised - and physically re-written - from the Cannons version of *Let God arise* (HWV 256a), and the central movements were entirely new settings of the Psalm verses concerned. The result was one of Handel's best anthems. In the outer movements the music from the Cannons version is tightened up and full use is made of the opportunities provided by the more extensive resources that were available for Chapel Royal services; the new movements comprise an ambitious dual aria for two of the Chapel's leading soloists, who then join together in a duet with a richly-scored accompaniment, where oboe and bassoon mirror the alto and bass voices.

The original vocal performers would have been the regular members of the Chapel Royal choir, probably no more than eight boys and a dozen men who were 'in waiting' at the time. From within the choir, Handel featured the leading voices of the alto Francis Hughes and the bass Samuel Weely as soloists, and he also made good use of musical interaction between the soloists and their colleagues to enrich and enliven the texture of chorus movements. The core of the accompaniment was provided by about a dozen string players from the King's Musicians, supplemented by some additional instrumentalists who were brought in specially. Payments in court documents record the employment of two double bass players (instruments which were not covered from the regular Musicians), the oboe player John Kytch and a bassoon player; most likely, Handel directed the performances from the organ. It is not certain whether the year for the performance of *Let God arise* was 1724 or 1726, though the latter is slightly more likely. The bassoonists were Richard Vincent in 1724 and Godfried Karpa in 1726: whichever of them was involved must have been an outstanding player, for the anthem and its companion Te Deum in A Major (HWV 282) contain the most interesting and extensive obbligato music that Handel ever wrote for the instrument. The Te Deum is also published in the Novello Handel Edition and the two works can be programmed together effectively.

SOME PRACTICAL CONSIDERATIONS
RHYTHMIC ALTERATION

Handel's notation is presented as the music text. Editorial suggestions for rhythmic modifications, indicated by 'flags' above the stave, have been added to cover two contexts: places where the last note of a phrase needs to be shortened in order to clear a harmonic change, and places where a rhythm may be amended to conform to the movement of other parts or the prevailing pattern.

MATTERS FOR SINGERS

In chorus movements the musical roles of the alto and bass soloists include strengthening the next-highest part. The alto parts (solo and chorus) can be taken by suitable male or female voices: the chorus alto parts occasionally have a low tessitura, especially at No 1 bar 33. In No 4 some passages require elision of a vowel on the repeat of the word 'hallelujah', shown as 'hal-le-lu-ja, hal-le-lu-jah'.

CONTINUO ACCOMPANIMENT

As is apparent from the music printed as small-size notes in the right-hand part of the accompaniment to this vocal score, some passages are accompanied by the basso continuo only, without upper orchestral instruments, though these passages are less extensive than in the airs from Handel's operas and oratorios. At the Chapel Royal the chord-playing continuo function for this work was performed by Handel on the organ, possibly a chamber organ brought in for the occasion rather than the Chapel's resident instrument. (This was the only chord-playing instrument involved, in contrast to his practice in theatre oratorios, where both harpsichord and organ were employed.) The Chapel Royal staff included a Lutenist, but the person concerned also had a place in the Musicians and would have performed in the string-orchestra ensemble instead.

The basso continuo obviously requires the participation of at least one chord-playing instrument. A fully-realised continuo part is included with the performing material of this edition, suitable for organ or harpsichord in present-day performances. The realisation follows the figuring from Handel's bass part, but this is very sporadic and the best guide lies in the harmonic implications of the music itself. A reduction in bassi instruments, to a continuo group of cello and organ (possibly with double bass), for passages accompanied by continuo alone, may not be necessary if modest instrumental forces are involved; editorial suggestions are, however, provided for this possibility when a larger orchestra is involved. This matter is discussed further in the Preface to the full score.

THE KEYBOARD ACCOMPANIMENT

Abbreviations at the beginning of each movement indicate the scoring, which in this work is identical for each movement.

The keyboard accompaniment is a practical reduction of the principal activity in the orchestral parts, suitable for rehearsal accompaniment. The harmonic bass line is preserved as the lowest part. Bracketed notes are used to show where one pitch is shared between two melodic lines.

'Senza D.B.' indicates orchestral passages without double bass, and 'Bassi' indicates subsequent re-entries; 'Cont.' indicates passages accompanied by the Continuo, including those where Handel's bass line shows the doubling of upper parts (usually chorus entries) without the participation of orchestral bass instruments. Editorial continuo realisation, shown in small-size notes, has taken account of Handel's intermittent continuo figurings. Indications for trills (from the sources, and editorial suggestions) are included, but all may not be practical for the keyboard accompaniment; in many places Handel's standard 'tr' marking indicates a short ornament.

SOURCES

i) HANDEL'S AUTOGRAPH SCORE

A London, British Library, RM 20.g.4, ff. 21-37. The final two leaves of Handel's autograph are lost: f. 37v ends with No. 4 bar 54. In the autograph volume, which was probably bound in the late eighteenth century, the anthem is preceded by the autograph of the A Major Te Deum (HWV 282), which was almost certainly composed as a companion-piece: the autographs are written on the same type of paper, and share the same soloists and characteristic scoring.

ii) MANUSCRIPT COPIES

B Manchester Public Library, Henry Watson Music Library, MS 130 Hd4 v.47(2). Full score, in a volume with the A Major Te Deum and the Chapel Royal anthem HWV 250b, copied by an unknown scribe, c. 1725-30. Unlike many other Handel items now at Manchester, this volume apparently did not originate from the 'Aylesford Collection'. It is an accurate copy from the autograph, apparently taken before the loss of the final pages, and includes the names of the singers.

C University of Chicago (U.S.A), Joseph Regenstein Library, U.S.A., MS 437. Part-books, vocal and instrumental, for Nos 2 and 3, occurring in nine books from the set, inserted within copies of the Cannons setting of the anthem (HWV 256a). From the 'Aylesford Collection'; originally copied by S2 for Charles Jennens *c.* 1740-5.[2] Jennens probably owned a score of these two movements, from which the parts were derived, and may not have been aware of the differences in the anthem's outer movements between the Cannons and Chapel Royal settings. The music in the part-books does not indicate an understanding of the performance circumstances for which HWV 256 was composed: the part-books for 'Violoncell & Bassone' contains only the bassoon music for No. 3.

D British Library, Egerton MS 2911, ff. 22-48 (original pagination 43-95), in a 'library' volume from the Granville Collection. Full score, copied by S1 *c.* 1740. An accurate copy derived from **A** and sharing some readings with **B**, but not including the singers' names.

E Cambridge, Fitzwilliam Museum MS 811, pp. 107-136, in a 'library' volume from the 'Lennard Collection'; the 18th-century spine label reads 'Anthems Vol II'. Copied by John Christopher Smith the elder, *c.* 1740-5. Smith was Handel's principal music copyist, but in this case his transcription is unreliable on account of his attempt to compress the score onto a limited number of staves.

Manuscripts **F-J** present the anthem in conjunction with the A major Te Deum, but derived both works from a defective source and have unreliable music texts.

F British Library Add. MS 29998, ff. 29v-51 (original pagination 56-99). Full score, copied *c.* 1725-30, possibly by Thomas Barnard. The original singers' names are included.

G London, Foundling Museum, Gerald Coke Handel Collection 1279, pp. 1-48. Full score, copied *c.* 1725-50, copyist unidentified. Bookplate of 'Messrs Sharp' from the later eighteenth century; subsequently owned by E. F. Rimbault.

H New Brunswick (New Jersey, U.S.A.), Rutgers, M2038.H14A5, vol. 2 (appendix), pp. 63-118. Full score, copied *c.* 1770 by S10, probably for Sir William Watkins Wynn.

J Foundling Museum, Coke Collection 1258. Full score, copied by Joseph Fish and dated 1770.

K London, Royal College of Music, MS 2254, ff, 29-48. Full score of Nos. 2 and 3 only, probably copied in the 1760s. Derived from the same defective source as copies **F-J**, and thus unconnected with **C**.

iii) PRINTED EDITIONS

W *The Complete Score of Ten Anthems Composed Chiefly for the Chapel of his Grace the late James Duke of Chandos by G. F. Handel …London Printed by Wright and Wilkinson* (1784), vol. III, pp. 416-446 (Anthem X'). This was the only Chapel Royal anthem in the three-volume anthology of Handel's anthems: the Cannons setting (HWV 256a) was not included. The presence of HWV 256b instead is explained by the circumstance that the copy-text for the publication was manuscript **E**, and the defects from that source were consequently repeated.

Ar1 *Anthem, in Score, Composed at Cannons, For His Grace the Duke of Chandos Between the Year's 1718 and 1720. By G. F. Handel* Samuel Arnold's edition, fascicles Nos 73 and 74 (*c.* 1790), 'Anthem II'. The music text was derived from **W** and reproduced its defects; the title page, used for each of the anthems, seems also to have been derived from the title-page of **W**.

Ar2 Title as for **Ar1**; Arnold's edition, fascicles Nos 73 and 74, 'Anthem III', pp. 18-26, 39-40. Unlike **W**, Arnold's edition included HWV 256a, into which Nos 2 and 3 from HWV 256b were inserted, repeating the music from **Ar1**. The coincidence with source **C** is remarkable, and Arnold may have known of the Aylesford material.

HG *Anthem XIb* in a vol. 2 of the collection of Handel's anthems for the Händelgesellschaft Edition, vol. 35 (1871), pp. 263-300, edited by Friedrich Chrysander. This avoided the errors from **W** and **Ar1**, but did not take into account the best sources for the closing section of No 4.

EDITORIAL PRACTICE

Handel's autograph (**A**) is the principal source for the complete anthem, apart from the ending to No 4 (bar 55 onwards), for which copies **B** and **D** provide an authoritative text. All other copies have been checked in detail but provide no significant additional contribution. The principal sources provide an accurate and comprehensive text: the few points requiring editorial intervention or interpretation are listed below, except for those that only involve only the instrumental parts, which are dealt with in the Preface to the full score. Movement numberings are editorial.

Clefs have been modernised for the vocal parts: the original clefs were soprano (C1) for soprano voices, alto (C3) for alto voices, and tenor (C4) for tenor voices.

Handel's system of accidentals has been modernised, and small-size accidentals are used where he may have omitted an intended inflection. The conventional long note in the final bar of No 4 has been retained. Note-beaming has been modernised. Handel used slurs in the vocal parts to indicate the word-setting, and these have been omitted, except in No 3 where they may also have been intended to indicate phrasing. Slurs in the orchestral parts from the principal sources are included, but obvious *simile* slurs and staccato dashes are not indicated as editorial unless there is some anomaly in the pattern; in the full score, all slurs that do not have authority from the principal sources are shown as editorial. The *hemiola*, or conventional cadential rhythmic re-grouping in triple time, is indicated by horizontal square brackets thus: ⌐ ¬ ⌐ ¬ ⌐ ¬ . Editorial suggestions for rhythmic modification are shown by 'flags' above the stave or stave-system: see above, 'Rhythmic Alteration'. Editorial suggestions for additional dynamics, tempo directions, staccato dashes, trills, etc. are shown in square brackets, and editorial slurs or ties are shown thus: ⌒ . Where, however, Handel indicated general dynamics incompletely these have been applied to all parts without editorial indication, and the same applies to the addition of *f* at the beginnings of movements to which Handel added *piano* in subsequent bars.

TEXTUAL NOTES

All listed readings relate to source **A**, unless otherwise noted. Additional details relating only to the orchestral parts are noted in the Preface to the full score for this edition.

No. 1
Bar

1 — No tempo marking in **A**; the Cannons version (HWV 256a) for this movement has *Allegro ma non troppo*.

15 — A solo: third note g′, making octaves with bass, but clear in **A** and copied in **B, D**.

27 — A chorus: first note altered by Handel from e′ to a′; **B** and **D** erroneously copy A solo for the whole of this bar.

38ff. — Handel wrote 'flee before him' in the Cannons version (HWV 256a), but 'fly before him' in this anthem; Psalm 68 in the *Book of Common Prayer* and the Authorised Version of *The Bible* has 'flee before him'.

49-52 — No naturals to the note G in **A**, but they are present in **B**.

57-8 — A solo: for the notes over the bar-line, Handel altered g′,e♯′ (as in A chorus) to b′, g′; copied as g′, g′ in **B** and **D**.

81 — A solo: first note g′, A chorus has ambiguous a′/g′, but Vln 2 has clear a′, and a′ in parallel HWV 256a.

82 — T: second note altered from f′: Vln 2 has a′, but a in T would have given fifths with bass, so Handel introduced a new chord.

NO. 2

30 — B: second note g in **A**; copied as a in **B** and **D**.

No. 3

21 — A,B: difference in rhythm on beat 4 between parts is clear in **A** and copies.

No. 4

9 ff. — Handel wrote 'halleluja' consistently at the first entries, but also 'halleluia', 'alleluja' and 'alleluia' subsequently in the movement; 'alleluja' at bar 39 A solo is not in Handel's hand, and was probably added by a copyist when preparing his own score.

35 — Handel wrote the accidental only to the last note of the bar.

54 — A solo, Vln 2: natural to g′ in **B**, but not in **A** or **D**.

55 — A solo: **B** (no autograph) has last two notes d′; but f′ in **D** and parallel Vla.

63-66 A,B: word-setting is editorial: no
       autograph, and the copies are
       unsatisfactory.
71-73 Written as two $\frac{4}{2}$ bars in **B** and **D**,
       with final chord as breve tied to breve,
       presumably copying lost autograph.

ACKNOWLEDGEMENTS

I extend my grateful thanks to the owners
and curators of the sources for this edition,
for facilitating access to the original materials.
Research for the edition, and initial preparation of
the music text by Blaise Compton, was supported
by the Arts Faculty at The Open University. I
thank those involved in the production of this
edition, in particular Howard Friend and Hywel
Davies from Novello Publishing.

DONALD BURROWS, 2010

1   For details of Handel's association with the Chapel
    Royal, and the music involved, see Donald Burrows,
    Handel and the English Chapel Royal (Oxford,
    2005).

2   For the 'S' classification of Handel's music copyists,
    see Jens Peter Larsen, *Handel's 'Messiah': Origins,
    Composition, Sources* (London, 1957), Chapter 4.

LET GOD ARISE

GEORGE FRIDERIC HANDEL
HWV 256

No. 1

Psalm lxviii, 1

Soli and Chorus LET GOD ARISE
Chorus with Alto and Bass soli

No. 2

Air LIKE AS THE SMOKE
Alto and Bass

Psalm lxviii, 2

Bars 2-4: Handel's slurring of semiquaver passages such as this, is inconsistent in this movement. He may have intended for this slurring to be used on corresponding passages throughout the movement.
*Handel wrote 'vanishes' here, but 'vanisheth' at bar 25.

- way, a - way, a - way, so shalt thou drive_____ them a-

- way. Like as the smoke,

[p]   pp   f

like as the smoke,

as the smoke van - ish - eth so shalt thou drive_____

Bsn

_____ them, so shalt thou drive__ them a - way, so shalt thou

drive___them a-way,   a - way,   a-way, so shalt thou drive___ them a - way,___

so shalt thou drive_____ them,

so shalt thou drive___them a - way,   so shalt thou   drive_ them a - way,___

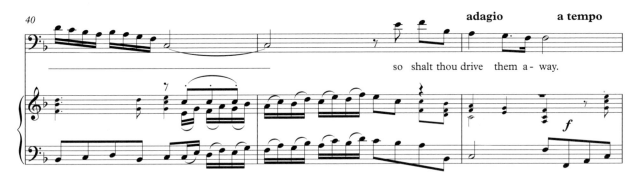

adagio   **a tempo**

so shalt thou drive   them a - way.

[Senza D.B.]

- - - - - - - - - ly per-ish at the

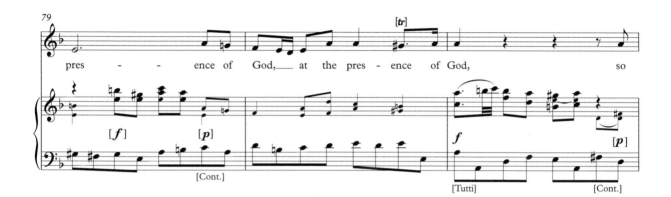

pres - - ence of God,___ at the pres - ence of God, so

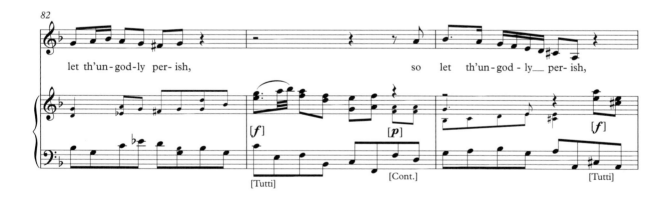

let th'un-god-ly per-ish, so let th'un-god-ly___ per-ish,

per-ish, per-ish, so let th'un-god - - - - - -

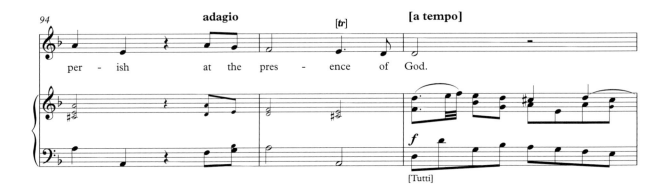

No. 3

Psalm lxviii, 4

Duet   O SING UNTO GOD
Alto and Bass

* See Preface concerning the slurs in this movement.

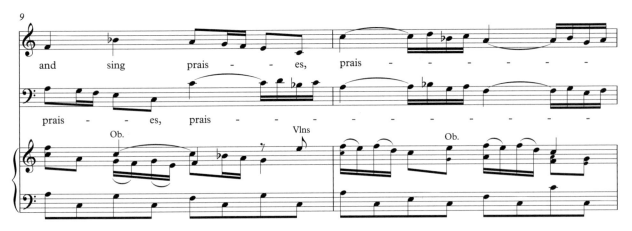

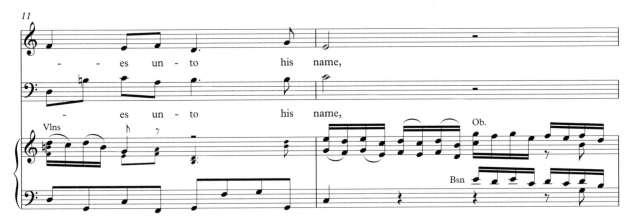

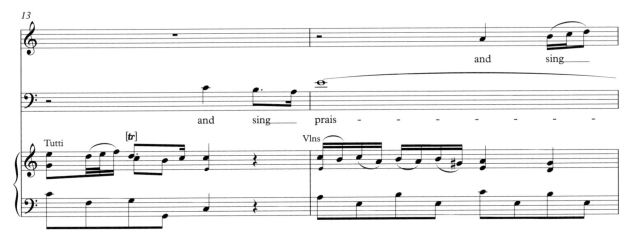

and sing prais — — es un — — to his

prais — — es, prais — es un — to his___

name, and sing prais — es, and sing prais —

name, and sing prais — es, and sing prais —

— — — — ses un — to his name.

— — — — ses un — to his___ name.

No. 4

Psalm lxviii, 35

Chorus with Solos BLESSED BE GOD
Chorus with Alto and Bass soli

[Senza D.B.]

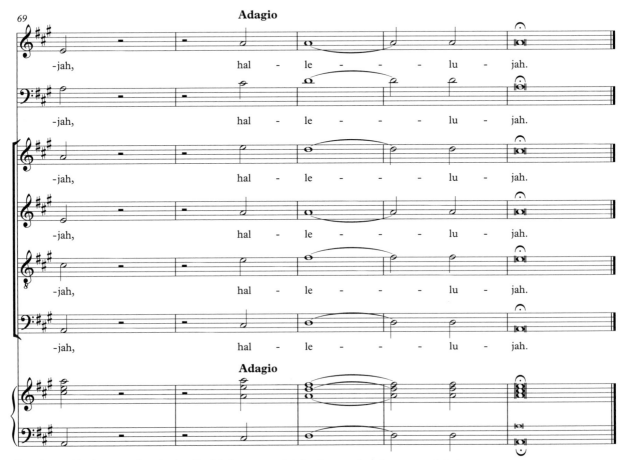

Bars 63-66, Alto, bass: word-setting is editorial: the autograph is lost here, and copies are unsatisfactory.